P9-BIP-262

START-UP
ART AND DESIGN

WHAT IS SCULPTURE?

Louise and Richard Spilsbury

Cherrytree Books are distributed in the
United States by Black Rabbit Books
P.O. Box 3263
Mankato, MN, 56002

Library of Congress Cataloging-in-Publication Data

Spilsbury, Louise.
   What is sculpture? / Louise and Richard Spilsbury. --
1st ed.
      p. cm. -- (Start-up art and design)
   Includes index.
   Summary: "Describes forms of sculpture, the textures
of materials used, and provides project ideas, including
wire sculpture and junk art"--Provided by publisher.
   ISBN 978-1-84234-525-2
   1. Sculpture--Technique--Juvenile literature. I.
Spilsbury, Richard, 1963- II. Title.
   NB1170.S65 2009
   731.4--dc22

                                    2007046393

13-digit ISBN: 9781842345252
10-digit ISBN: 1842345257

First Edition
9 8 7 6 5 4 3 2 1

First published in 2007 by Evans Brothers Ltd.
2A Portman Mansions, Chiltern Street,
London W1U 6NR, United Kingdom

Produced for Evans Brothers Limited by
White-Thomson Publishing Ltd.

Editor: Rachel Minay
Consultant: Susan Ogier Horwood
Designer: Leishman Design

Acknowledgments:
Special thanks to Ms. J. Arundell and pupils at Mayfield
Primary School, Hanwell, West London, for their help
and involvement in the preparation of this book.

Picture Acknowledgments:
Alamy pp. 5l (The Photolibrary Wales), 14 (Mike
Kipling Photography), 20 (Jenny Matthews); Bridgeman
Art Library pp. 8t, 16; Corbis pp. 5r (Richard T.
Nowitz), 6 (Bruce Burkhardt); Chris Fairclough pp.
cover (all), title page, 7l&r, 9l&r, 11, 13t, 15, 17 (all),
18l&r, 19, 21; iStockphoto.com p. 12 (all);
Shutterstock.com p. 4.

Artwork:
Amy Sparks p. 13b; Tech-Set Ltd. p.10.

Contents

What Is Sculpture? 4

Sculpting People 6

Animal Sculptures 8

Cardboard Construction 10

Art from Nature 12

Junk Art 14

Casting Sculptures 16

Sculpture School 18

Sculpture Settings 20

Further Information for Parents and Teachers 22

Index 24

What Is Sculpture?

A **sculpture** is a work of art.
It is often a **solid** shape,
not flat like a painting.
Some are huge;
others are tiny.

◄ This sculpture is called *The Angel of the North*. It is 66 feet (20m) high—that's taller than ten grown men!

sculpture   solid

Sculptures are often made of strong materials, such as metal, stone, or wood. But they can be made from all kinds of materials.

▲ How long do you think this ice sculpture might last?

◀ We can see sculptures in galleries, town squares, parks, and even our homes.

materials   galleries

Sculpting People

Sculptures of people take many different forms. French sculptor Auguste Rodin made structures that are solid and life-size or larger.

◄ What emotion does this figure's pose suggest? If he could talk, what do you think he would say to you?

sculptor   life-size   emotion

"I pressed the feet into clay to make my figure stand up."

▲ Joe's class is going to make wire sculptures of people in different poses. The children take photos of each other. How will this help them?

► The children twist and bend wire into people shapes.

pose   twist   bend   clay   7

Animal Sculptures

► This is a sculpture of a stalking wolf. How does the sculptor make the wolf look as if it is moving?

How would you describe this sculpture in a letter to a friend to help them imagine it clearly?

► Zoe's class makes a spider diagram about the sculpture. What would you add to it?

black — shiny
color
long
thin legs
shape
muscly
Stalking wolf
how it feels
cold
smooth back
sharp ears

spider diagram   models   sketches

The children make clay animals. They look at models and draw sketches to help them make their sculptures more realistic.

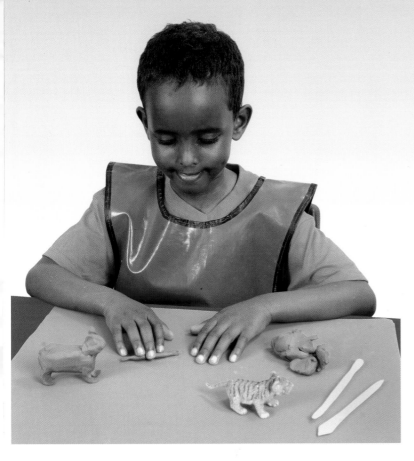

▲ They make a clay body and then add the head and legs. James is rolling out a tail for his tiger.

▲ Zoe presses tools into the surface of the clay to make a pattern for her cheetah's back.

realistic   tools   surface

Cardboard Construction

Sculptures are formed by putting different shapes and spaces together in particular ways. Ben and his class construct a sculpture from different pieces.

Cylinder   Cuboid   Circle

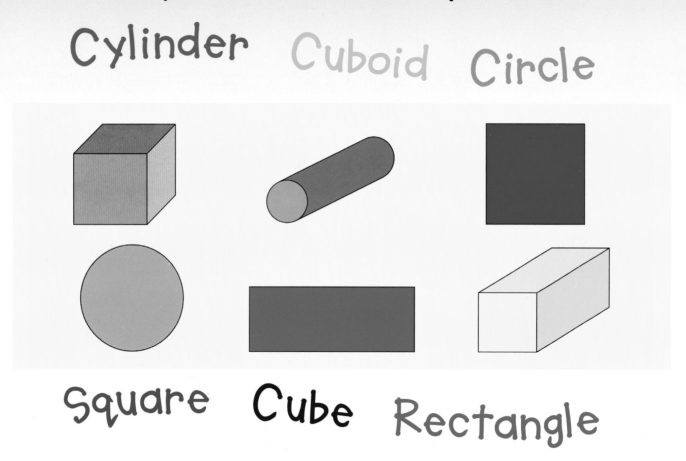

Square   Cube   Rectangle

First they make geometric shapes out of cardboard. Can you match the words to the shapes?

construct   geometric

The children think carefully about where to put the pieces. They try the shapes in different positions to create an interesting and balanced sculpture.

▲ The pieces in this sculpture are joined together with glue. What other methods of joining can you use?

positions   balanced   joined

Art from Nature

Nature makes sculptures, too! The sea carves sand, wood, and shells into interesting forms.

sand and seaweed

driftwood

shells

▲ How would these natural sculptures feel to touch?

Tip: When you are out, collect some natural objects for a sculpture, but only take fallen or dead materials.

12

carves   forms   research

▶ **Max and Neela research the artist Andy Goldsworthy. He often uses natural materials such as leaves and petals. Why does he take photos of these temporary sculptures?**

◀ **Neela made her own temporary work of art. She made a relief collage by arranging natural objects on cardboard.**

temporary   relief collage

13

Junk Art

▶ This sculpture is made from reclaimed parts of electronic equipment. It represents the electronic waste one person makes in a lifetime.

How much waste does your family throw away each week? How much do you reuse or recycle?

reclaimed   represents   waste

▼ Dominic's class collects used materials for a sculpture. They make a junk art dragon.

wire and old fabric

old CDs

cereal boxes

egg box

What other reclaimed items did they use? What kind of junk sculpture will you make?

reuse   recycle

Casting Sculptures

Every culture makes sculptures of some kind. This bronze head was made in Africa around 500 years ago.

▶ Big bead necklaces were only worn by royalty. The head is wearing a crown. The crown has strings of valuable beads too.

Sculptures like this are made by casting. Casting means making something in a mold.

culture   bronze   casting

Katy is making a cast sculpture. First she presses shapes into clay with tools and objects such as shells. These are her molds. Next she will pour plaster into the molds.

► When the plaster sets hard, the sculpture is taken out of the plastic tray. Katy paints the sculpture to look like bronze.

mold   plaster   sets

Sculpture School

Sculptures can brighten up surroundings. An artist helped this school make a sculpture trail in the grounds.

◀ One class used the theme "Africa." Individual pieces were painted and joined together to make totem poles.

▶ This lion was made from clay. The features were carved while the clay was wet.

theme   totem poles   features

▼ The school also made a willow installation. Willow canes were planted in the ground and then bent and woven together to make an igloo and tunnel.

How do you think the sculptures improved the school environment?

installation   environment

Sculpture Settings

Many sculptures are **displayed** in galleries. In a gallery, you can look at a sculpture from different **angles**.

▶ How do you think it feels to stand beneath this sculpture?

displayed   angles

It is useful to talk about how you feel about your own and other people's work. One sculpture can **communicate** **different** **ideas** to different people.

Further Information for

New words listed in the text:

angles	construct	geometric	plaster	research	surface
balanced	culture	ideas	pose	reuse	temporary
bend	displayed	installation	positions	sculptor	theme
bronze	emotion	joined	realistic	sculpture	tools
carves	environment	life-size	reclaimed	sets	totem poles
casting	features	materials	recycle	sketches	twist
clay	forms	models	relief collage	solid	waste
communicate	galleries	mold	represents	spider diagram	

Possible Activities

PAGES 4-5

The children could sort 2D and 3D objects to help them think about the differences.

Think about why different materials are used. When visiting outdoor sculptures, children should think about why metals such as bronze are used (long-lasting). What might weather do to outdoor sculptures?

PAGES 6-7

To help them with their wire sculptures, children could look at the wire figures of Alberto Giacometti. How do the sculptures make them feel? What are the figures doing? How does the fact they are modeled in wire give them a very different feeling from Rodin's solid sculptures?

PAGES 8-9

The children could think about why artists choose particular materials to work with. They might choose wood, so they can make certain marks in it or cut it in a certain way. Children could also discuss ways of getting inspiration and background material from which to work. They could visit a zoo, take photos or make sketches of animals, or study other animal sculptures for ideas. Many sculptures are carved, not modeled. At http://www.tate.org.uk/learning/kids/zoomroom/soapcarving/ there are ideas for making a soap sculpture based on Barbara Hepworth's sculptures.

PAGES 10-11

Children could first work in pairs to make sculptures out of plastic linking shapes. When making an abstract sculpture, be clear that when artists create an apparently random form they actually make many careful decisions about the end result and experiment before welding or joining the pieces together. You could look at the work of American sculptor Alexander Calder, who used shapes and colors to make interesting abstract sculptures. Children could work individually on a sculpture like this, using materials such as lollipop sticks, pipe cleaners, and straws.

Parents and Teachers

PAGES 12-13

When on a nature walk, the children can think about what they can smell and see, and the textures they can feel. At the beach or woods, get the children to make ephemeral pieces of art themselves, such as sculptures made of sand or piled leaves. This could lead to discussions about the beauty of our fragile world, and how nature is constantly shifting and changing. Children could also make a nature mobile from found items such as driftwood, twigs, shells, and cones. They will need to think about balance and symmetry to make the mobile work.

PAGES 14-15

Under supervision, children could take apart or use dismantled washing machines and other electronic equipment to make their own version of the WEEE sculpture.

Children could make a sculpture from reclaimed materials to stand near a recycling station to encourage people to think about recycling and to cover up unsightly bins.

Children could explore some of the sculptures Picasso made using junk items, such as a monkey with a toy car for a face.

PAGES 16-17

Viewing sculpture in relief on buildings could help with the cast model work. This could also link with a science project, such as one on skeletons, as children could use (clean) animal bones to create molds too.

PAGES 18-19

For an interesting fact sheet about willow sculpture and how to do it, see: www.schoolsgarden.org.uk/resources/20willow.pdf

PAGES 20-21

If possible, arrange a visit to a gallery, ideally with the help of a gallery guide who can offer the children some insight into the

sculptures and suggest new ways of seeing the art on display. This will also help the children think about the way they display their own sculptures and the significance of naming the sculptures. At the gallery, they could think about what questions they want to ask about a piece, such as why an artist chose a particular medium, and think about giving visitors to their own gallery this kind of information. The children could take photos of their sculpture work and load them onto the school web site themselves, with descriptions of the processes involved and their feelings about the projects.

Further Information

BOOKS FOR CHILDREN

Sculpting (Action Art) by Isabelle Thomas (Raintree, 2005)

What Is a Sculpture? (Art's Alive) by Ruth Thomson (Franklin Watts, 2005)

Cranium Super Sculpting (A Play It Again Book) by Inc. Cranium (LB Kids, 2007)

ArtLab: Clay Studio by Julia Harrison (Becker & Mayer, 2007)

The Life & Work of Auguste Rodin by Jayne Woodhouse (Heinemann, 2001)

The Life & Work of Henry Moore by Sean Connolly (Heinemann, 2001)

WEB SITES

www.artsconnected.org/classroom/

http://www.tate.org.uk

http://www.nga.gov/exhibitions/caldwel.htm

http://rb043.k12.sd.us/wire_sculpture1.htm

Index

b
bronze 16, 17

c
casting 16, 17
clay 7, 9, 17, 18
cultures 16

e
emotions 6
environment 19

f
forms 12

g
galleries 5, 20
Goldsworthy, Andy 13

i
installation 19

j
joining 11

m
materials 5, 12, 13, 15
models 9
molds 16, 17

n
nature 12

p
photos 7
plaster 17
poses 6, 7

r
recycling 14
relief collage 13
research 13
Rodin, Auguste 6

s
sculptors 6, 8
sculpture trail 18
shapes 4, 7, 10, 11, 17
sketches 9
spider diagram 8

t
temporary sculptures 13
The Angel of the North 4
themes 18
tools 9, 17
totem poles 18

w
waste 14
willow 19
wire 7